Transformed by His Love

A True Story of Love, Loss & Forgiveness

KEN AND LEONA KLASSEN

To my God, my King,
my Lord.

To Ken, the love of my life.

To the readers to know the love of God,
receive it and be transformed.

Table of Contents

Preface

These poems were usually written early in the morning and sometimes after waking from sleep with a word or thought and a deep desire to write.

For some time I've felt an intense urgency to write. There is a great need for us as the Church to awaken because the Bridegroom is coming. I don't know the time or the hour, but now is the time to awaken, to walk in one accord as His Church. We are called to have an intimate relationship with Abba Father. To seek and know His Heart, to bring heaven to earth, to be a brilliant light in this darkness and be a beacon of love, hope and grace in this fallen world. There is so much more to life than what we've known.

As our life unfolded, I felt the Lord impressing upon me to share our story (intertwined with poems). Life is a gift! Thrive, beloved thrive!

It is my prayer that these words will ignite a flame and a passion that cannot be quenched. We are His, our lives are not our own, it is time to repent, to surrender all. Repentance has come to mean to me: to change or examine our direction, resulting in a stirring of our hearts to action.

May Abba Father keep you and bless you!

Hallelujah, Hallelujah, Hallelujah,
Amen, Amen, Amen!

Transformed By His Love

A True Story of Love, Loss & Forgiveness

KEN AND LEONA KLASSEN

Crucify Him, They Chanted

The pounding echoed throughout the crowd
Blood dripped from where the spikes were set to rest
The tree plunged into the ground, jolting the body upon it
Blood trickled down from where the crown of thorns sat.

A "King" it read from above the condemned man
Criminals hung on both sides, one mocking,
the other believing
Faces blurred as they spat and ridiculed the dying man
At His feet the casting of stones over pieces of cloth
could be heard.

Hours passed, the sky now black though still day
As if the sun turned its face away, not able to witness
the scene below.

The man cried out, giving His last breath
In the distance the curtain was torn
The earth rumbled as if in pain, mourning the death
of its Creator
Tombs were opened and the dead walked.

The innocent man, yet not man but the Lord
Died to free us from our chains of bondage
Though death could not keep our Lord,
For He dwells in every one of His children.

***

I found this poem in a box of pictures, cards and letters. This poem was written when Ken and I started writing to each other.

We met in our early 20s but as life goes we kept passing each other until friends of ours decided to play matchmaker, for which I am forever grateful. We started writing, because Ken had moved to BC and I was still living in Saskatchewan. Those love letters, a thing of the past, are now so precious to me. We married on Nov 10, 1990, with hopes and dreams for the future. We were so young and carefree, eagerly looking forward to this new adventure together. We had no idea that the twists and turns that would touch our life together were bent on tearing us apart. But the choice was still ours. Right from the beginning we chose to make our marriage a covenant with God. Divorce was not an option.

Awaken

Awake, dear child awake
My love and mercy surround you
Look to Jesus, take My hand,
And walk with Me
My gift I freely give to you,
Rise up and walk in My grace

Arise, dear sons, arise dear daughters
You are My work of art
In Christ you are alive
Loved, adored and blessed
Walk in my love
My grace is sufficient

Dream, My child, dream
I have a plan for you,
For your unique self
A purpose, for you to grow and thrive
With gifts to prepare your way
Rise up and walk in My grace

Look up, My beloved, look up
From your wounded brokenness
Take My hand and find rest
My love overflows for you
Be renewed, be restored
My grace is sufficient

Live, blessed one, live
Let Christ's power flow
You are redeemed
Shower the world with My love
Let your light shine
Rise up and walk in My grace

Rise up sons, rise up daughters
Well done, My faithful ones
You have finished the race
Join with Christ in the heavenly realms
Celebrate, dance, you are free
Run, jump and praise My Holy Name

***

As I wrote this poem, I was studying a Scripture verse and the words poured out of me. At that time Ken and I had been married for over 31 years. I think that by sharing some background, I can help shed light and understanding before I share the rest of our story.

Ken was born into a Christian family, the eldest of four children. At the age of seven Ken received Jesus into his life and knew he was to be a pastor. There was a deep calling upon his life. As life goes, it's not always so simple or predictable. Ken's school years were hard. Between being bullied and not fitting in it was a lonely time for him. For a short time during those years he hung out with a group who influenced him negatively. He got into trouble and was exposed to pornography which is a very common struggle for men. Porn is an addiction used by the enemy to shame and cripple our potential to serve the Lord. To add to that, Ken struggled with wondering whether God loved him and, if he messed up, was God angry with him? This belief is so far from the truth. This is something Ken struggled with off and on throughout his life. His living in shame and self-condemnation caused him to become a prisoner of his own making and living in the past impacted our future. As our life together unfolded, we realized, though not soon enough, how the enemy attacks those that are a threat to him. Ken was a threat.

Then there is me, Leona. I grew up going to church only occasionally. We lived on a farm and I loved being out in nature and as I grew it became my comforting sanctuary. However, there was a darkness lurking in the shadows of my childhood. During this time I was also exposed to porn. Fear, lost innocence and too many secrets were buried inside me. Through it all and despite everything, I was still a free spirit. I knew that I was loved by God, that God was love. God's hand was upon me and He had a plan for me even though I didn't know it then. When I was 12, my family moved from the farm to be closer to the city. This is when I chose to go to church even though my family didn't. At 13 I received Jesus into my life, which was the best decision I ever made. I can't imagine living life without my Lord.

As you can see, Ken and I came from very different backgrounds, each with our own set of baggage. After we married, we talked about breaking the cycles that we grew up with. However, sometimes we get distracted and forget what's really important. The foolishness of the world distracts us from the wisdom of the Father.

In a nutshell, we were blessed with four children, three boys and a girl, and sadly lost two babies preterm. Ken worked as a drywall contractor for a lot of those years, but also managed to return to Bible school to complete his bachelor's degree in Strategic Ministry. He pastored for several years and we moved many times, living in three provinces. In later years we also dabbled at small-scale farming, owned a lot of different animals and enjoyed being out in nature again.

During our first year of marriage

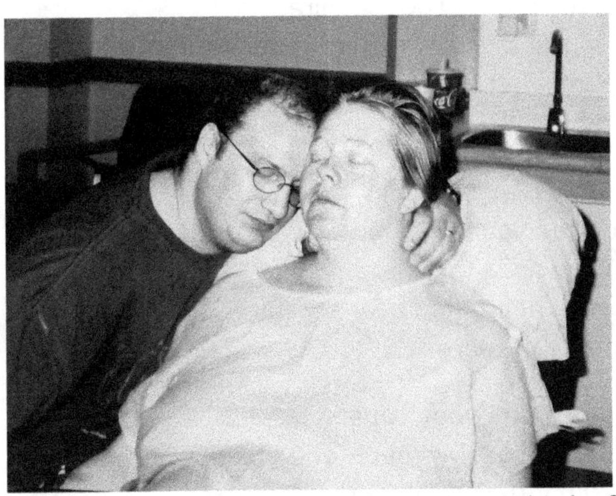

*Ken never left my side during the traumatic birth of
our third child*

Remember Who I AM

Awaken, dear lost ones
My scattered stones come back to Me
I will bring healing to your mind, body and soul
Open your eyes, listen to my voice
Remember who I AM

My beautiful children
I formed you in your mother's womb
I wove you with love, care and joy
You are created unique with great purpose
Remember who I AM

Beloved sons, beloved daughters
Open your eyes to see the miraculous
My loving kindness surrounds you
My creation declares My Holy Name
Remember who I AM

My children
Awake from your slumber,
Now is the time, take a stand
Open your heart, and hear My voice
It is time to prepare

Repent beloved ones, repent
Know I Am good, My mercy and grace abounds
Take My hand, and follow Me
I will give you rest, hope and a future
Remember who I AM

Arise sons, arise daughters
Be renewed, be revived, I will redeem you
Be filled with My Spirit in My authority and power
With your lips sing praises to My Holy Name
Live in victory, knowing I will supply all your needs

Remember and Know I AM, Jehovah, the Alpha and
Omega, Almighty God, King of Kings, Lord of Lords,
Prince of Peace, Emmanuel, Holy One
The battle is won! Nothing is impossible with ME
Be My beacon of love and hope to the world.

***

As in any marriage we had our ups and downs, but the
later years or were the most challenging of our lives.
We had stopped going to church. We were wounded,
hurt and felt so alone. We didn't know where to turn.
Our family was imploding. Each of us was hurting and
angry, handling the emotional and spiritual turmoil in
our own way. We were bombarded by the enemy, under
attack from all directions, broken and crushed. We had
lost our way, forgotten who we were and believed the
lie that we were failures; that our lives didn't matter. We
struggled with feeling we weren't good enough. We felt
we'd messed up and therefore God must be angry with
us. This greatly impacted our lives and our marriage.

Beloved, do not grow weary for your lives do matter, you do have a purpose! Jesus is right beside you walking with you through the fire, and on many occasions He is probably carrying you. Beloved, rest in His love, lay your burdens down and never forget you are HIS child, HIS masterpiece, HIS beloved!

***

Ah, Lord God! Behold, You have made the heavens and the earth by Your great power and outstretched arm. There is nothing too hard for You.
Jeremiah 32:17

And do this, knowing the time, that now it is high time to awake out of sleep; for now our salvation is nearer than when we first believed. The night is far spent, the day is at hand. Therefore let us cast off the works of darkness and let us put on the armor of light.
Romans 13:11-12

***

For You formed my inward parts;
You covered me in my mother's womb.
I will praise You, for I am fearfully and wonderfully made;
Marvelous are Your works,
And that my soul knows very well.
My frame was not hidden from You,
When I was made in secret,
And skillfully wrought in the lowest parts of the earth.
Your eyes saw my substance, being yet unformed.
And in Your book they were all written,
The days fashioned for me,
When as yet there were none of them.

How precious also are Your thoughts to me, O God!
How great is the sum of them!
If I should count them, they would be more in number
than the sand;
When I awake, I am still with You.
Psalm 139:13-18

I Hear Your Cries

I hear your prayers and see your anguish
I have promised never to leave you or forsake you
You are My son, My chosen one
I AM Your Abba Father

I see your pain and suffering
I AM your comfort, your strength, your refuge
Know I walk beside you every step of the way
You are My beloved, My precious son

I see your heart and longing to serve
But you struggle in silence with shame
and self-condemnation
Son, you are forgiven, your sins washed away
I have you in the palm of my hand

Take My hand, find rest
Know My heart, be filled with peace
My favour and blessing are upon you
My son, I love you

***

Sometimes in our life's journey, we can get so stuck and trapped that we feel there is no way out. We don't know what to do and we're frozen, fearful of being judged or criticized. We keep going, just surviving as the days turn into years and before we know it our life has passed by and we are left feeling empty and alone. Don't let the lie of the enemy become so deeply rooted that it takes dying to finally realize the truth. Cry out, yell, scream out your frustrations and your struggles to God and wait for Him to work, because there is so much more to life than just surviving! There really is only one choice to make: Life or Death.

***

Cast your burden on the Lord, and He shall sustain you; he shall never permit the righteous to be moved
Psalms 55:22

Then they cried out to the Lord in their trouble, And He saved them out of their distresses.
Psalm 107:19

Fear not, for I am with you; Be not dismayed, for I am your God. I will strengthen you, Yes, I will help you, I will uphold you with My righteous right hand.
Isaiah 41:10

Remember Who You Are

My chosen people, know Me
Hear My voice, listen to My Spirit
I Am calling you
Open your heart to know Me
My abundant love, and mercy surrounds you
Remember who you are

You are My beloved creation
Lift your eyes to see Me
I formed you, created you, You are mine
Hear Me now, you are blessed
You are adopted and redeemed for purpose
Remember who you are

Repent sons, repent daughters
Know you are forgiven
The past is washed away, forgotten
Time to stand and live in freedom
I call you a saint
Remember who you are

Rise up above the ashes
You are my workmanship
Created in My image
To live carefree, filled with joy
With a song of thanksgiving on your lips
Remember who you are

My beloved, you are set apart, holy
You are called, watchman to stand at the gate
Praising My Holy Name in worship
Praying, fasting and declaring My word
In My power and authority
Remember who you are

Remember, you are beloved
Forgiven, restored, and redeemed
You are made holy, My blessings are upon you
You are a Royal Priesthood, a Holy Nation
Created in love in My image, made with a plan
A purpose to be fruitful as My co-worker
Go, live in peace and victory!

*But as many as received Him, to them He gave the right to
become children of God, to those who believe in His name.*
John 1:12

*For we are His workmanship, created in Christ Jesus for good
works, which God prepared beforehand that
we should walk in them.*
Ephesians 2:10

Time To Prepare

Awaken My church, awaken
My scattered stones come together and unite
A darkness is growing across the land
Stand and believe, the time has come
Shake off your slumber and arise
Repent and be revived, renewed and healed
Hear My call, prepare

Now is the time, My chosen ones
The enemy is on the prowl, ready to devour
Fast, pray and worship My Holy Name
Sing songs of praise, shout out My decrees
Declare My word in power and authority
It is finished, walk in victory
Hear My call, prepare

My beloved children, arise
Hear My voice, know My heart
I long for all to be saved
Pray with Me in one accord
Be filled with My joy and thanksgiving
Knowing that I Am with you always
Hear My call, prepare

My precious sons, My precious daughters
I long for you all, to be of one mind in Christ
To submit to each other, to move as one

Love each other as I have loved you
My favour and blessings are upon you
Go, be a blessing to all
Hear My call, prepare

My adopted heirs, My children
Be bold and be courageous
Live loved, walk in freedom
I give you everything you need
To overcome and subdue the enemy
Know My miraculous deeds
Hear My call, prepare

My children, I call you righteous
Know My voice, obey My words
I long for relationship with you
Be baptized with My spirit
Walk in My wisdom and truth in victory
I AM your refuge, your strength
Hear My call, prepare

Stand, My children, you are a Holy Nation
The harvest is ready, but workers are few
You are My sons, My daughters
Your life is not your own, you are called by name
Follow Me and be My vessel of mercy and hope
You are called a Royal Priesthood
Go, making disciples in all nations

***

I am so thankful for Ken! He was a good hardworking man who was dedicated to doing the job well. I loved these things about him, and also how he loved people and made friends wherever he went. Ken had such a big heart but there was a darkness that consumed him. In later years the wounds compounded and the enemy's lies became real to him. Ken thought, "How could God love me? God must be angry with me because I failed again. I messed up, I can't seem to do anything right." Ken even asked me if anyone would care if he died.

I now understand that Ken didn't want to burden me with his struggles. By protecting me from them, he was loving me. So he stuffed them down and hid his pain. There were times when Ken did confide in me, and it drew us closer together and I loved him even more. But as the darkness grew, his silence was deafening. The dreams he had and the ones we shared died. What he didn't realize was that his pain was leaking out through his actions and manifested in frustration and anger. I knew there was something driving a wedge between us.

Beloved, men were created to protect and love their families. But in the trials and wounds of life, perspective can become distorted. A man doesn't always know what to do and his mindset becomes tainted. Displaying love becomes difficult as deep struggles with shame and condemnation get suppressed. But there's also a strong desire to not hurt or burden loved ones.

Beloved, when one is hurting, the other will also suffer. You are either a blessing or a curse to each other. You are one, bound together in a covenant. Your dreams and your life are intertwined with each other. Beloved, you have a choice. Choose to love each other well. True love takes sacrifice and giving of self as you look to the cross.

And be kind to one another, tenderhearted, forgiving one another, even as God in Christ forgave you.
Ephesians 4:32

Thank You Jesus

Long ago as the prophets foretold
A child would be born from a virgin
The Messiah would come from the line of David
To walk among His people, His creation
Thank You Jesus, for coming to save me

The child grew up a man, yet God
Perfect, with no sin or defect
A sacrifice to end all sacrifices
All for His beloved children
Jesus, thank you for Your abundant love

Jesus grew in strength and stature
He walked in obedience, in prayer
Doing His Father's Will
To be the Saviour for all people
Thank You Jesus, for choosing to walk among us

Our Jesus gathered His disciples together
Loved them, taught them, and healed the sick
Jesus poured His life into His people
To bring Salvation to the world
Jesus, thank you for saving us

The religious hated their Messiah
He was rejected by those He loved.
The Chosen One, mocked, spat upon and beaten
Stripes that left His body torn and bloody
Thank You Jesus, for Your sacrifice

They hung God's Son, our Saviour, on the tree
A crown of thorns on his head
Nails pierced His hands and feet
While they mocked Him, Jesus forgave them
Jesus, thank you for saving my soul

A darkness filled the land
Jesus cried out, yielding up His Spirit
The temple veil was torn in two,
The earth quaked, saints were raised from the dead
Thank You Jesus, for giving Your life

In three days the temple would be raised
Jesus was dead, but now is alive forevermore
The power of sin is broken
He revealed Himself and walked among them
Promising that He was with them always

He could have called 12 legions of angels
But willingly chose to be our Salvation
Endured so much more than we could comprehend
With unconditional love and forgiveness
My Saviour, My Lord, thank you!

***

In that dark period of our lives we lost hope for a while.
We felt so alone, with no support and no community.
We were struggling to survive and didn't know how to

move forward or what to do. I had become angry and frustrated at Ken and at life. I became numb, my tears dried up, and one day ran into another. Ken wasn't the only one repressing feelings.

During that time, I came across a picture online that revealed the ugliness of bitterness. In that picture an elderly woman was purposely inflicting pain on her bedridden husband by intentionally clipping his nails to the quick, causing them to bleed. His expression was of sadness and pain. The look of pure delight on her face as she did this was so horrendous that it shook me to the core. I did not want to grow old and become that person! That was the beginning of fighting the darkness and letting go of anger and resentment. It was the beginning of finding my way back to God and finding out who I was. I began to find purpose in my life again and to fight for my marriage; to fight for Ken and not against him.

Sowing seeds that tear down are creating wounds that bring discord, whether in the name of fun or through venting, is a sin. Those seeds can grow to kill dreams, destroy relationships, and even worse, drive people away from God. We are called to walk in unity, loving one another. When one part of the body suffers, the whole body suffers. Words have the power of life or death.

***

Let no corrupt word proceed out of your mouth, but what is good for necessary edification, that it may impart grace to the hearers.
Ephesians 4:29

And if one member suffers, all the members suffer with it; or if one member is honored, all the members rejoice with it. Now you are the body of Christ, and members individually.
1 Corinthians 12:26-27

Fear My Holy Name

Dear children, My beloved
You have forgotten My commands
Your love has grown cold and you don't fear Me
Love without fear is dead
A darkness is growing, the time is near
Fear Me who can destroy both body and soul to hell
Seek Me and I will draw near to you

Remember My chosen ones
I created the foundations of all life
The earth declares My mighty deeds
I give you every breath you take
Every moment of your life is a gift
I created you, wove you
To have a relationship with you

My scattered stones, awaken!
Repent, and renew your mind
Search for Me as a lost treasure
Stand in awe of Me, and declare My Holy Name
Humble yourself and seek to know Me
Work out your salvation in fear and trembling
For this brings healing to your body and soul

Sons, daughters I AM calling you!
I will supply you with everything you need
Know My Holy Spirit and listen
He is your companion to guide you
Every moment of every day

Know His voice and obey
Everyday He longs to hear your voice

My children, My Holy Nation
I AM the Alpha and Omega, the Lamb of God
Deep reverence is the fountain of life
Great is My loving-kindness, My mercy
For with honor comes wisdom
To perfect the holiness in each of you
With love and fear, I can now call you friend

***

On this journey I've come to realize that love is not enough. We can love God but if we don't have a holy reverence for our Lord, falling into sin and drifting away becomes too easy. Every aspect of our life can fall apart when we don't fear the Lord. I now better understand more the depth of agony Ken was hiding. He felt tortured and was suffering. Ken loved the Lord. We both did, but we didn't fear Him. We spent too much time living in fear instead of fearing and being in awe of our Lord, not understanding the intensity of the Father's love for us, and not open to receiving it. The price is steep when you walk in death but thanks be to God, He is the Redeemer! Beloved, choose Life!

Our Father

Our Father in Heaven
Holy is Your Name
Your Kingdom – **COME**
Your Will – **BE DONE**
On earth as it is in Heaven

Sons of Abraham, ARISE
I Am calling you, lead My people
Sons of God, be My holy warriors,
Stand, be men of honor and valor
Victory is in My hands

Holy, Holy is my Lord God Almighty
The earth trembles at Your voice
You are my rock, my fortress
Glorify Your Holy Name
You are my God, my King

Daughters of Sarah, AWAKEN
I Am calling you, trust in Me
Arise beloved, be courageous, be strong
Walk in a gentle and quiet spirit
For I Am with you always

Holy, Holy is my Lord God Almighty
Blessed is Your Name
You are my refuge and strength
May Your praises flow from my lips
You are my God, my Lord

May each house declare – **WE WILL SERVE THE LORD**
For multiple generations to come
Walking in obedience in His power, truth and love
God's blessings will overflow
May our lives bring glory and honor to You Lord

El Shaddai, Lord God Almighty
Yahweh, Lord Jehovah
Yours is the Kingdom
The power and glory forever
Amen, amen, amen

***

We moved in the spring of 2018 to a rural community closer to Saskatoon. In 2019 my mom died and we had some other hardships that broke our hearts. In Spring 2020 my dad died and we experienced the stress of dealing with the estate. During this time we decided to find a church family again. In searching for a family of believers, God led us to a small church in February 2021, which changed our lives. We learned there was so much more to the Christian life! How the Holy Spirit is crucial to walking in the Father's love and in knowing His heart. We had been living far below our purchase price! Christ died and was resurrected so we may live life abundantly, not just survive. We were working through our brokenness. Ken had a hard time receiving the Father's love and forgiveness. I was fearful, still working out who I was and I didn't realize how much it was affecting me and my marriage.

Beloved, let go of the past for it will destroy your future. Don't waste any more time. Beloved, choose life and life abundantly. Be a blessing to each other and thrive. Live, love and walk in unity with each other, reflecting the Father's heart. Seek His wisdom and be carefree, knowing He will provide all your needs. Beloved, you are called. Take up your Sword of Truth and fight. Be the Warrior you were created to be!

On October 13, 2021 I sent this message to Ken, "I love you Ken and I want the best for you and our marriage." Ken replied, "I know that it is hard to see, but there are some things that are changing on the inside. I love you too." Our hearts were starting to mend, as we looked more and more to Jesus. It felt like we were starting to live again. Ken and the guys were doing men's breakfasts and golfing. We were hanging out with friends and meeting new people.

In June 2022 Ken's mom passed away. Ken was so thankful that he was able to fly down to BC to see her before she died. In Spring 2023 our daughter and her family moved closer so we could now see our grandsons. In June, all three of our sons were baptized, which was such a joyful event! Ken's dad remarried in December, and we were happy for him, but there was also a sense of loss for all of us, especially for Ken. Ken longed for a deeper relationship with his dad but that was not to be. Sometimes we keep looking to our earthly father for things that only Abba Father can provide.

***

Then he said to them, "Go your way, eat the fat, drink the sweet, and send portions to those for whom nothing is prepared; for this day is holy to our Lord. Do not sorrow, for the joy of the Lord is your strength."
Nehemiah 8:10

But You, O Lord, are a God full of compassion, and gracious, Longsuffering and abundant in mercy and truth.
Psalm 86:15

Mercy

Mercy, mercy, mercy
El Shaddai, Lord God Almighty
So many lost ones
No one to tell them the Good News

Heavenly Father, forgive us
For we have lost our way
We have forgotten who we are
And the voices of the lost go unheard

Mercy, mercy, mercy
Yahweh, Lord Jehovah
Awaken us, so we can hear Your voice
Unite us, heal our brokenness

Lord Jesus, forgive us
We have forgotten the price You paid
Rejected, beaten and whipped beyond recognition
Hung on a Cross, a criminal's death

Mercy, mercy, mercy
Adonai, Lamb of God
The blood of the lost is crying out
Revive us, restore us, redeem us

Holy Spirit, forgive us
For we have ignored and grieved You
We have denied the power of Your gifts
While nations go without a Lord and Saviour

Mercy, mercy, mercy
Jehovah, Lord Most High
Fill us, baptize us with Your gifts
To walk in obedience in Your mercy, hope and love

***

In April 2024, Ken planned to take me to the city for the weekend to celebrate my birthday. I was so surprised! Deep down I feared something would happen and it wouldn't work out, so I didn't even book a hotel until several days beforehand. It turned out to be a really great weekend - we spent much needed time with each other. Our relationship had been up and down for years, and now Ken was making a greater effort to do things for me. It did not go unnoticed but I, too, was struggling with feeling numb. I hadn't cried, really cried, in many years. Earlier when I voiced this to Ken, he said, "We will get through together, I love you." I so loved Ken, but fear still held me captive.

During this time we were in the planning stage of building a garage and loft. We really needed the room and having a garage would be wonderful for Ken. But as we worked through the details, our financing fell through. We were a bit shocked and surprised but Ken sensed that it was for the best, that somehow it would have hindered us in the future.

On June 18, 2024 I texted Ken, "I was thinking about you, I am so blessed to have you, my handsome one, in my life." Ken responded with, "So glad I married you." There were some very difficult things happening around us that last year, but we were continuing to come together. Ken was struggling with health issues as well. Between Ken's health and the various challenging situations, it was taking a heavy toll on him.

Ken continually surprised me. We like animals and were thinking about purchasing a milk cow. I like making butter and cheese – which probably sounds crazy to most people but I enjoy it. When I mentioned a particular cow for sale to Ken, he took the day off work and drove me to see her. Actually it was more like *getting* the cow! On our drive home Ken kept emphasizing that "Minnie" was *my* cow. He took the time to do this for me because he knew how important it was to me. Another special memory to hold onto!

Ken

Life had been hard. In the last year things had escalated. I was feeling alienated by certain people I cared about, shame consumed me, my head was in a fog, and I wasn't feeling well. I became even more depressed. Being around people used to energize me but now it drained me. It was becoming harder and harder to keep up appearances that everything was okay. I was dying inside and I kept trying to distract myself and numb the pain. I was watching too much TV, scrolling on my phone and listening to stuff that just drew me further from God. When your wife comments that you're spending more time with your phone than with her, you know something's wrong. I even stopped reading, something I really enjoyed. Sometimes at work I couldn't hold it in anymore and I would sit and cry. "If I can't work, who am I without drywall?" My life was out of control, but Leona was trying to find ways to help me feel better. She would sit quietly beside me; her presence was soothing. I don't think she fully realized how comforting it was to me. She encouraged me to dream, to make a list of things I wanted to do. But I was empty and I didn't know what I wanted anymore. I was stuck and it felt like there was no way out. Throughout, Leona was a safe place to fall.

My Comforter

Holy Spirit, forgive me
I have lived too many years,
Not really knowing who You are
Walking blindly, grieving you

Have mercy on me, Holy One
I need you, open my eyes to see you
Guide me, to hear Your voice
My soul thirsts for Your rivers of living water

The cry of my heart is to know You!
Holy Spirit fill me, baptize me, transform me!
I long to pray together in one accord,
In Your tongue

Spirit of truth, I love You
I yearn for Your thoughts, to be my thoughts
For Your dreams, to be my dreams
Teach me Your ways

Thank You, Holy One of God
You are my comforter, my companion
How Great is Your gentleness, and compassion
You are a Mighty Warrior

Holy Spirit, You are welcome
May we walk in harmony,
Moment to moment of everyday
May my life be forever surrendered to You

Thank You, Spirit of Truth
For I will be baptized and gifted
With what's needed to walk this journey
For this is a promise and Will of God
Amen, amen, amen

***

On this journey with God, He is leading us to know Him more and that He, Abba Father, wants an intimate relationship with us. He is not an angry God who delights in punishing us, but we are His children, His beloved. We are blessed with the gift of the Holy Spirit who is with us every moment of the day to guide us on this journey. We had drifted too long in the foolishness of the world. Thank you Lord, for showing us that wisdom only comes from you.

Daughters of Sarah

Daughters of Sarah, AWAKEN
Be still and know I AM Jehovah
I have created you with purpose
Woven you each uniquely
Rise up and be courageous

Daughters of the Most High
Remember who I AM
El Shaddai, El Elyon, Adonai
Know Me, trust Me
I have a plan for you

My Daughters, I hear your cries
I see your anguish, your confusion
Surrender all, and I will give you rest
Know My hope, peace and joy
I have you in the palm of My hand

My beloved Daughters, ARISE
From the ashes, restored, and renewed
Remember who you are, precious
Created in My image, worthy and holy
Rise up and be free

Daughters, walk in love
Nurture those that I have brought to you
Do not be swayed by feelings, for they are deceptive
My words bring LIFE, My Spirit will guide you
I AM with you always

Daughters of Sarah, open your eyes
Marriage is a covenant, sacred
Meant to increase your ability to serve
To expand both of your lives, yet be in one accord
Beauty comes from a gentle and quiet spirit

Daughters, I AM calling you to serve
Your husband is My son, be in awe of him
Be thankful for him and you will be blessed
All you need is ME, I AM El Shaddai
Trust ME, for I AM good and faithful

***

In writing these poems, so much has been about what I am learning and what the Holy Spirit is impressing upon my heart. My prayer has become "Lord create in me a gentle and quiet spirit." I've been learning to go to Father in prayer about everything and letting Him work things out. In my marriage there were times when I tried to help but I only made the situation worse. Only after I had exhausted my attempts at fixing the issues did I finally turn to God. God knew better than me and He knew exactly what Ken needed. He waits and longs for us to give all to Him. God's will is always perfect.

***

To know ABBA Father
is knowing His word
To know Jesus, our Lord and Savior
is opening your heart in repentance
To know the Holy Spirit
is walking each day in harmony with Him
In knowing the Trinity, you will be
empowered and filled with truth in love
In our obedience, we will be
a beacon of hope and mercy to the nations.

***

With this next poem, I was awoken at 5 am with the word "storm" so strong in my mind and such an urgency to write! This poem flowed word for word with one of the strongest messages. I had a strong feeling that time was of the essence. Abba Father is calling His children to awaken NOW. Beloved, the time is now to seek Him with all your heart, mind and soul. *WE* must prepare!

***

For the word of the Lord is right,
And all His work is done in truth.
He loves righteousness and justice;
The earth is full of the goodness of the Lord.

By the word of the Lord the heavens were made,
And all the hosts of them by the breath of His mouth.
He gathers the waters of the sea together as a heap;
He lays up the deep in storehouses.

Let all the earth fear the Lord;
Let all the inhabitants of the world stand in awe of Him.
For he spoke, and it was done;
He commanded and it stood fast.
Psalm 33:4-9

Hear My Voice

My children hear My voice,
A storm is brewing
Will you weather the storm with Me or without Me?
A darkness is growing, overtaking the land
Are you ready?

My people, I AM here
I said I'd never leave you nor forsake you
Awaken before it's too late
Repent and be revived, renewed, and redeemed
Be ready for the battle that's coming

My sons, My daughters, bow before Me
Stand at the gate in intercession
Fight for your heart and mind, for your loved ones,
your community, the nations
You will walk through the valley of the shadow of death
Will you be crippled in fear or walk in My victory?

My children, know My heart
Be thankful in everything, praise and fear My Holy Name
Walk in obedience, in one accord with the Holy Spirit
Accept the gifts I have for you, live empowered
Then My peace that transcends all understanding
will surround you

My people hear Me NOW
Time is fleeting, the enemy has blinded you,
too many distractions

I Am calling you, repent
Draw near to Me and I will draw near to you
Stand, know Me, so you can know who you are in Me

My beloved, you have drifted from Me
To know Me, is to know My word
My word is alive and the breath of life
It will wash over you and restore your soul
Thirst for My word and you will be transformed

My sons, My daughters
Take up the Cross and follow Me
Time is fading away
Without Me, your life will grow cold
Repent dear children, REPENT

My beloved sons, daughters
Will you weather this storm?
Will you allow fear to destroy you?
Stand My children, I Am your refuge, your rock, your shield
Walk in thanksgiving, praise and worship,
then you will overcome this world

My children, the CHOICE IS YOURS
Obey Me or be overtaken
I have never left you, My love and grace surround you always
Will you take My hand...
And walk with Me or walk against Me?

Ken My Beloved Son

I Am calling you
Come to Me and lay your burdens down
Awaken My son, believe
For I AM with you always
I AM creating a good work in you
Repent, My son, and arise

Ken, I created you
You were woven with purpose
A destiny to lead My people
Yield, My son, seek to know My heart
A fresh revelation I will give to you
That will pierce the heart, bringing conviction to many!
Deny yourself, pick up the Cross and follow ME

Ken, I have you in the palm of My hand
I AM building a firm foundation under you
on the Rock of Christ
You are bound together with the bride of your youth
Side by side you will stand, unstoppable
A covenant that will not be broken
What the enemy did to destroy you, I AM redeeming!
In your room, come together, pray and worship Me

Ken, My beloved son
I Am calling you, shepherd My people
My breath is upon you, be healed, be renewed
The hunger inside you will grow, never to be satisfied
with where you're at
I will drive you, deeper, deeper, deeper into MY presence
I Am pouring onto you wisdom and revelation
from the heavens
Just because I love you!

Ken, blessed one, you are holy
You will walk through the valley of the shadow of death
But don't be afraid, for I AM with you
I Am giving you divine courage,
Boldness, and strength in speech
In this season My bride will be awakened!
My hand is upon you, be empowered!

Ken, My beloved son
You have squandered your time,
Keeping Me at arm's length
These hardships are meant to refine you, to prepare you
Seek Me, take My hand ... time is fleeting!
For you will be fruitful and a blessing to all those around you
I AM calling you now, shepherd My people

***

This is a poem I wrote for Ken - words that were spoken over him the last couple of years. We need to be an active participant in our transformation, yielding to Father's plan for us. By our choices we will either help or hinder that process. Beloved, do not be seduced by the world! Protect your eyes from what you watch and read. Protect your ears from hearing words that speak death upon you. Protect your heart from the wounds of life and forgive or you will drift away. Beloved, choose Life!

***

And do not be conformed to this world, but be transformed by the renewing of your mind, that you may prove what is that good and acceptable and perfect will of God.
Romans 12:2

Being confident of this very thing, that He who has begun a good work in you will complete it until the day of Jesus Christ
Philippians 1:6

Ken enjoying digging a hole for the watering bowl for the animals. So thankful Ken got that done. 2023

Warrior's Heart

Abba Father, search my heart
Renew a right spirit within me
Clothe me with humility
That I may walk in Your peace and joy
Overflowing with Your love and grace

El Shaddai, Adonai
Blessed is the name of the Lord
O Lord, breathe upon me, revive me, redeem me
That I will walk in freedom
Empowered to be a beacon of hope to the nations

Yahweh, Elohim
My Creator, My King, My Lord
Thank you for forming me in Your Image
Creating me unique with a purpose
In Your book my name and destiny are written

Abba Father, hear my cries
O Lord, I surrender all
Transform me to love, as You have loved me
To walk in obedience, faithful to You
To be a child of promise

Jehovah, El Elyon
Praise the Lord all my soul
Fill me, baptize me with the Spirit of Truth
Open my ears, my eyes, my heart
May Your praises flow from my lips forevermore

Lord God Most High, Alpha and Omega
Who is, who was, and who is to come
May I walk in Your power, and authority
To stand, to fight, to intercede
A warrior to serve You, my King, my Lord
Amen, amen, amen

***

It's your choice, are you a Warrior for your King, or a prisoner of war of the enemy?

Throughout the last year, actually for much longer than Ken would admit, he had been more tired, experiencing more aches and pains and he had been losing weight without trying. But when you work hard in a very physical job that comes with the territory. Ken kept working; it's what men do. The pain continued to get worse until it was difficult to work. During that time it was hay season and Ken fixed equipment and swathed and bailed hay. We finally went to the emergency room at the local hospital on August 20, 2024. The doctor who saw him thought he was suffering from kidney stones. She sent Ken home with instructions to come back for an ultrasound the following day. That day changed our lives forever. The ultrasound revealed Ken had a large growth on his kidney. They didn't say it was cancer, but that was the implication. Next we waited for appointments, and a CT scan which they said could be weeks away! Ken's pain progressively grew. He was not sleeping in bed with me anymore. He couldn't lie horizontally, so he slept in an office chair. Ken's pain was not managed; he was coping by trying to keep his mind busy or distracted. I was trying to do anything I could to make Ken more comfortable. Watching Ken in such pain was one of the hardest things I had ever done. Helping and caring for him was the easiest choice ever. Ken was the love of my life. No matter what had been said or done, he was my husband, my love.

The pain increased so we went to a hospital ER in Saskatoon. There they did the CT scan immediately and recommended to the surgeon that Ken get an appointment as soon as possible. Over a week later we sat in the surgeon's office and our life changed in an instant. We thought Ken would have the surgery and everything would be good – cancer gone – but that was not to be. The doctor told us that the cancer had spread, that Ken could live a couple months, maybe years, if treatment worked. You hear news like that and you're in shock; it's hard to comprehend. Ken chose surgery even with all of the risks it posed. He thought that once he had recovered he would have a break from the pain and then fight the cancer with whatever therapy we chose. On September 16, 2024 Ken underwent surgery. It was very difficult. The tumour had grown substantially and it really was a miracle that he survived and I could have more time to spend with him. I was so thankful to be able to love and care for him a little longer; although, in my mind and in my heart I was believing in a miracle.

The Lord gave me these verses during this time. *Proverbs 3:5-6 - Trust in the Lord with all your heart, and lean not on your own understanding; In all your ways acknowledge Him, and He shall direct your paths.*

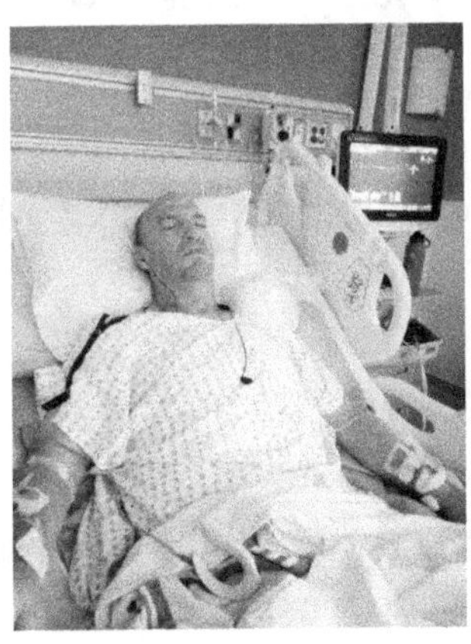

Cry of Your Heart

Oh My children, My sons, My daughters
Hear My voice, I Am calling you
From your wilderness look up to Me
In the storms of life, seek Me
For I Am with you!

In your brokenness cry out to Me
I Am Almighty God, Abba Father
Open your heart, release your agony
Cry out from the depth of your soul!
For I Am listening

I do have a purpose, a plan for you
Fall to your knees and repent
For I love a humble heart
My child, pride leads to destruction
Come to Me and lay your burdens down

In your cries, a power is released
You are being healed from deep within
You are in My hands, and I Am always working
For I have deposited in you, something which is
unique only to you
Come to Me, and I will give you rest

My beloved, My children
As you walk this journey, let pain be your teacher
Know that there are no mistakes, for I Am the Redeemer

You are created in My image, in My likeness
To bring My Kingdom to earth
Know Me, I Am Abba Father, I Am Love

***

As Ken recovered in the hospital, I wasn't allowed
to stay overnight and Ken was really struggling. One
evening Ken called me after the doctor had stopped
in. I was on my way to Bible study. He phoned me
and told me that the doctor had told him that he had
only months left. We were both crying and I couldn't
believe that Ken was alone when he received the news.
When I got to church I just sobbed in my friend's
arms and our pastor prayed. I kept thinking that I
needed to get to Ken - I couldn't allow him to be alone
anymore. I mentioned it and my friends said they had
a few things to do and then they would take me to the
hospital. By the time we arrived it was midnight. We
prayed and walked in past security, to the elevators, up
to the fourth floor and all the way to the end of the
hallway. Nobody tried to stop us. Ken was overjoyed to
see me and I was so thankful to be there! I stayed
by his side until Ken went home. I am so thankful for

how Abba Father answered our prayers and provided for our needs.

Several times we visited our daughter and her family in their home. Despite Ken's pain and discomfort during the drive, seeing them was extremely important because he loved them all so much! He could do little but sit in a chair and he'd nod off but it was important to just be present. During this time our sons were busy maintaining our homestead. We were so thankful for their willingness to step in and we were very proud of them.

At home Ken was slowly recovering, but sleeping in a bed became an issue again so Ken basically lived in an office chair. It was the only chair that felt comfortable because of the constant pain he was experiencing. Often throughout the day Ken would stand leaning forward against the couch and I would rub his back to help relieve the pain. I did what I could to help. Touch was so very important. It was amazing how it calmed Ken. At other times I moved a kitchen chair beside Ken and held his hand. There were times I would nod off and wake as I fell forward, but Ken held me, keeping me from falling. We spent so many hours every night listening to praise music, watching shows, sermons, praying, or reading to Ken until he could sleep some more. This is how our nights looked during those months. Ken had a few days where he was starting to feel better, then things changed. The pain got worse and Ken couldn't keep any food down. During this time Ken looked at me and said "Leona, you do realize I could never have done this without you?" I just looked at Ken, frozen. Fear gripped me. I was trying so hard to be strong for Ken, to not fall apart. I didn't want to make things harder on him. I didn't want Ken to die. We were supposed to grow old together, but life wasn't going the way we'd planned.

By the beginning of November, Ken's health was growing increasingly worse. His brother came to visit from Vancouver Island. At this point Ken could still walk but couldn't keep any food down. I'm thankful that Ken got to spend those days "gallivanting around the countryside," eating his favourite creamy soft serve ice cream (even though he knew it wouldn't stay down), just spending time with his brother and an evening watching the Grey Cup game on TV. That time meant so much to Ken. They had always been close, but life got busy and they didn't see each other as often as Ken would have liked. We learned to never take anything for granted, live life intentionally, spend time with people and do things that are important to you.

As we were leaving our home for the ER one of the final times, to address the constant vomiting, Ken leaned against the wall to steady himself in the entryway. He looked at me in anguish. I think he believed he would not be coming home again, and the fact he was dying tore him apart. Ken had me promise to convey to all our children how much he loved them and how proud he was of them.

You have armed me with strength for the battle; You have subdued under me those who rose up against me.
Psalm 18:39

Have you not known?
Have you not heard?
The everlasting God, the Lord,
The Creator of the ends of the earth,
Neither faints nor is weary.
His understanding is unsearchable.
He gives power to the weak,
And to those who have no might He increases strength.
Even the youths shall faint and be weary,
And the young man shall utterly fall.
But those who wait on the Lord
Shall renew their strength;
They shall mount up with wings like eagles,
They shall run and not be weary,
They shall walk and not faint.
Isaiah 40:28-31

The Perfect Sacrifice

In days of old priests sprinkled blood seven times
in the Holy of Holies
Atonement for the sins of Yahweh's people
Foreshadowing things to come
To bring salvation and freedom to all mankind
The perfect sacrifice to end all sacrifices

In the Garden of Gethsemane Jesus knelt
In sorrow and distress He prayed "not My Will,
but Yours, be done"
Jehovah sent an angel from Heaven to strengthen Him
Earnestly Jesus continued to pray as sweat became blood
and fell to the ground.
The first shedding of blood

In the darkness, betrayed by a kiss
Our Lord was taken by a multitude with swords and clubs
The priests and elders condemning Him to death
They mocked, spat at, struck and plucked out His beard,
and beat our Yeshua
The second shedding of blood

From Pilate to Herod they mocked the Lamb of God
They held Him in contempt and put a fine robe upon Him
Herod and Pilate found no fault in Jesus to deserve death
But Pilate had our Lord scourged, His body
shredded and bleeding
The third shedding of blood

His own people cried out "crucify Him"
The soldiers took our Lord and mocked Him
Stripping Him, putting a scarlet robe upon Him
Striking the twisted crown of thorns they put
upon Christ's Head
The fourth shedding of blood

Our Precious Lord, so beaten and unrecognizable
They led Him to be crucified at Golgotha,
the place of the skull
They laid our Jesus, the Lamb of God upon the Cross
Pounding heavy spikes through His hands
The fifth shedding of blood

It read The King of the Jews above His head
They pierced His feet, nailing them to the Cross
As they crucified our Lord, they continued to mock Him
The soldiers cast lots for Jesus' clothes
The sixth shedding of blood

Criminals hung on either side, one mocked,
the other believed
Jesus cried out "Forgive them, they know not what they do"
Darkness fell upon the land, He cried out "It is finished"
and yielded up His spirit
The soldier took a spear, pierced Jesus' side,
and blood flowed
The seventh shedding of blood

The earth quaked, graves were opened and the dead walked
The veil in the temple was torn top to bottom
The shedding of blood seven times completed
the final sacrifice
On the third day, our Lord was raised and walked
the earth again
Restoring our relationship with Him

My King, My Lord, Praise Your Holy Name
Words cannot describe what You did for us
You brought us from death to Life
Freed us from our bondage, no longer separated from You
My King, My Lord thank you for saving our souls
Amen, amen, amen

***

On November 7, 2024 Ken received this letter from a friend from church who had asked God, "What message or word do you have for Ken?"

"I love him, I care for him, he is My beloved son. I admire his courage. He has been faithful to Me throughout his life and this period of life is no different. Beloved, Beloved, beloved, he is My beloved. This period of life that he is going through is a trial, but it is not ME. I am not punishing him for anything. What he's going through is not a punishment. I love him. I have good plans for him that he will accomplish."

Life is hard, but it's a gift. We tend to be so hard on ourselves, thinking we need to live perfect lives, but Abba Father sees our hearts. We will stumble and sometimes fall, but He is always there, waiting for us to take His hand. Jesus is right there walking with us through the fire. Father longs for us to seek Him, love and adore Him, to know His heart. The more we know Him, the more we will know who we are in Him. His love will overflow from us to all those around us. No matter what is happening, we are Abba Father's beloved sons and daughters. We are adopted and heirs to the Kingdom. Beloved, choose Life.

***

The steps of a good man are ordered by the Lord,
And He delights in his way.
Though he fall, he shall not be utterly cast down;
For the Lord upholds him with His hand.
Psalm 37:23-24

He heals the brokenhearted, and binds up their wounds.
Psalm 147:3

Follow Me

My beloved children hear Me **now**
I created the heavens and the earth
When sin entered, decay and destruction rippled
throughout My creation
Know My heart, we had a plan
A plan to bring you back in fellowship with us again
Believe, My beloved, believe
Follow Me

My sons, My daughters, I AM calling you!
The Lamb of God, My faithful Son
Was born, walked this earth in obedience and shed His blood
Dying on the Cross and rising again
Bringing all things back to order
The perfect sacrifice to end all sacrifices
Repent and Follow Me

Oh my wayward children
Open your eyes, open your ears, open your heart
Hear My voice and tremble
For I AM, Almighty God, Adonia
You are in the palm of My hands
Repent, be renewed and walk in freedom
Follow Me

My children, you have forgotten
The price that was paid for your ransom
My beloved Son, your Saviour, your Lord

He came, suffered a criminal's death
From sweating drops of blood while praying
To being beaten and scourged beyond recognition
Repent and follow Me

My children, My creation
Awaken before it's too late
My voice has been echoing throughout time
The earth cries out My Name
My Son is the way, the truth, and the life
NO ONE comes to ME, except through HIM
Follow Me

My children, hear Me
The time is growing shorter, darkness overcoming the earth
Listen to My voice, take My hand
I love you, created you in your mother's womb
You are unique, made with a purpose, your story
written in My Book
I will provide for all your needs
Follow Me

My children, Arise and be My Holy Nation
Walk in My power, My strength, My courage
For I have overcome this world
Stand beloved, and let My love and grace pour
from your broken vessel
"I AM the Alpha and Omega, the beginning and the end
who is, who was and who is to come, the Almighty" Rev. 1:8
Follow Me

✳✳✳

After several trips to the ER, Ken ended up in the Saskatoon hospital again. After tests and assessment, he ended up in palliative care, which actually became an amazing week for us. The care was exceptional and the time together was healing. The day we went into palliative care, and I mean "we", I stayed at his side. It was November 10, 2024, our 34th wedding anniversary. Ken with the help of friends bought me a gift. I threw my arms around him and then opened it to find a beautiful necklace, silver hearts intertwined. This is something I will always treasure. In spite of all of Ken's pain, and the fact that it would literally take a miracle to survive, he gave me this final gift.

A pastor friend, prompted by the Holy Spirit, came to spend time with Ken to help him work through his struggles. It was between me and the love and support of our church that Ken fully realized he was God's beloved son. Sometimes we don't know or understand the depth of the Father's love for us. We can be so wounded from past hurts that our hearts become hardened. It can be difficult to receive love even when it's right in front of us. Ken now realized Christ was always there, walking through the storms with him. He turned to God recognizing and accepting the Father's love. Ken's true heart and longing was revealed. He forgave himself and the peace of God filled him. He finally realized he was free, and the look on his face was priceless. To see my Ken so at peace was such a gift! I threw my arms around him and we cried together. Ken told me how much he loved me, another memory to treasure!

Beloved daughters don't ever underestimate the power of your love for your husband. Father gave me everything I needed to love Ken throughout this journey, in spite of my own brokenness. As I look back I'm amazed how I did it, with months of little sleep, staying in the hospital with Ken and just watching him fade away. Father gave me the strength, the courage and the love to care for Ken in those last months that we had together, and to do it with a grateful heart.

Many precious things happened that week. Ken was finally able to rest in bed and his sleep improved. He was still uncomfortable and it was awkward with the IV and the nasogastric tube going down his nose to drain his stomach. Ken would invite me to crawl into bed and snuggle next to him. One night we were able to make it work and we fell asleep in each other's arms for one last time. This is another memory I will always treasure. That week Ken was stronger, and even walked down the hall, so we went home to fight the good fight.

During this time the Lord gave me this verse I Thessalonians 5:18, "In everything give thanks; for this is the will of God in Christ Jesus for you."

Ken had many family members and friends come to visit during his time in the hospital. His dad and sisters coming to see him was especially meaningful since he rarely saw his dad and visits with his sisters were even less frequent. The visits from our daughter and her family were also a highlight. With them now living closer to us, reconnecting was such a blessing and time spent with our grandsons was very precious! They are such amazing little boys who had captured Ken's heart (and mine) and we have several dear pictures of the boys snuggled in Ken's arms. Our sons visits meant a lot to Ken. Two of our sons had birthdays that November and Ken was so thankful to be able to celebrate with them.

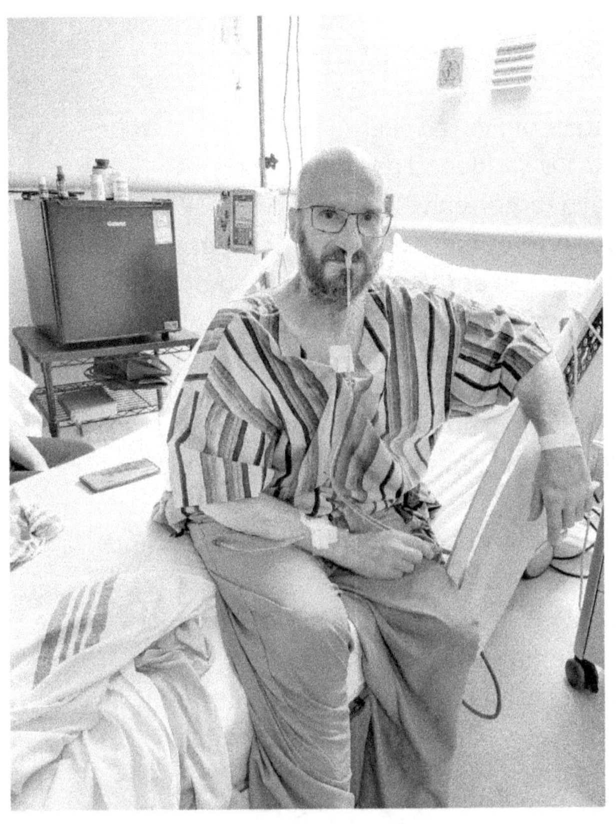

Therefore submit to God. Resist the devil and He will flee from you. Draw near to God and he will draw near to you.
James 4:7-8a

The righteous cry out, and the Lord hears,
And delivers them out of all their troubles.
The Lord is near to those who have a broken heart,
And saves such as have a contrite spirit.
Psalm 34:17-18

Awaken, Daughters of Eve

Daughters of Eve, awaken
My heart is saddened as I look upon you
You have forgotten who you are
You believe yourself to be victims, oppressed by man
You fight to be equal and better than one other
You have trapped yourself in a prison of your own making
Oh daughters, for you have lost the race.

My daughters, you have lost your way
The competing, the complaining, the criticizing
of each other
This journey is not about you and your feelings
It is a race; be a people of honor
Where MY love and mercy overflow onto all
those around you
It's about resting in Me, trusting I will supply all your needs
Awaken, beloved ones before it's too late

Awaken, daughters I AM calling you!
Stop the discord among yourselves
Your appetite for control brings decay to
the depth of your soul
Your words have become like a poison that spreads
like a cancer
Stop blaming each other and take responsibility, for this
is not about you!
Look to the Cross, and remember the shedding of blood
Repent! Beloved daughters, repent!

Arise from the ashes, daughters of Sarah, arise!
Hear My voice and obey, fear My Holy Name
You are created uniquely, there is no one like you!
Rest in Me, know My heart, I have a plan for you
You win by your conduct, being pure in heart
By the beauty of a gentle and quiet spirit
For this is precious to Me

Daughters of the Lord Most High, life is a gift
Know you are loved, so be My Love
Know you were created with purpose, so walk in freedom
Trust Me, believe, I have you in the palm of My hands
Walk in courage, in strength with forgiveness engraved
upon your hearts
Loving all people, seeing them through My eyes,
echoing these words
"Forgive them, for they do not know what they do."

Daughters take My hand, and be redeemed
You were bought with a price, you are not your own
There is a darkness, but remember I have
overcome this world
I Am calling you to be at peace with all mankind
Beloved, I have so many blessings I long to shower upon you
Trust Me, and know I will never leave you nor forsake you
May your heart cry, "Not my will, but Yours, be done!"

***

For some years Ken and I struggled to find the depth of relationship we had once enjoyed with each other and with God. Too often we got distracted and offended by one another or by others which took away from our relationship. We focused on our feelings instead of on the truth. The difficult times outweighed the good memories, and we almost forgot how good we were together. We let hardships and the enemy control us, and we drifted for too long. We talked but we didn't really communicate and work through the difficult issues. Fear held us captive. In spite of everything we chose not to give up on each other. True love is a choice, a daily decision to stay and work through whatever challenges are before you. I am grateful that Ken chose to love me in spite of his brokenness and shame (and mine). If there is anything I would pass on it is this; love your man with such a deep passion that it could only come from the Father. Look at him through Christ's eyes. Your man is a prince in exile, a son of the Lord God Almighty! You are blessed. Father has a plan for him, a purpose. Trust the Lord, who knows all things, to work that out in him.

Ken

Things that happened when I was a teen set the stage for the rest of my life. A moment in time can change your life forever. Sometimes I struggled with things but it wasn't until later in life that the past consumed me, giving the enemy a foothold in my life. I lived with regret and pain for the choices I had made. Whenever things became really stressful, the shame and condemnation from the past filled me, smothering me. I was drowning. How could God love me with this darkness inside of me? How could anyone? So I put my head down, threw myself into my work and just survived. When I was faced with dying, I realized I was out of time. The years had gone and I hadn't really lived, I had only existed. I had dreams and best intentions for Leona and for my kids. But my time was coming to a close. I had spent too much of my life not forgiving myself and not embracing God's love for me. I was a wounded man walking. I lived in brokenness. I was so focused on past sins, that had already been forgiven, instead of living and enjoying the blessings God had given me. Life is too short! LIVE! Accept God's grace, forgive yourself and know that God loves you more than you can comprehend. Jesus is walking with you throughout the storms of life every step of the way. Take Jesus' hand and never look back! Walk in His victory and live!

***

*Blessed be the God and Father of our Lord Jesus Christ, the
Father of mercies and God of all comfort, who comforts us in
all our tribulation, that we may be able to comfort those who
are in any trouble, with the comfort with which we ourselves are
comforted by God.*
2 Corinthians 1:3-4

*But now, thus says the Lord, who created you, O Jacob,
And He who formed you, O Israel:
"Fear not, for I have redeemed you;
I have called you by your name;
You are Mine.
When you pass through the waters, I will be with you;
And through the rivers, they shall not overflow you.
When you walk through the fire, you shall not be burned,
Nor shall the flame scorch you.
For I am the Lord your God,
The Holy One of Israel, your Savior*
Isaiah 43:1-3a

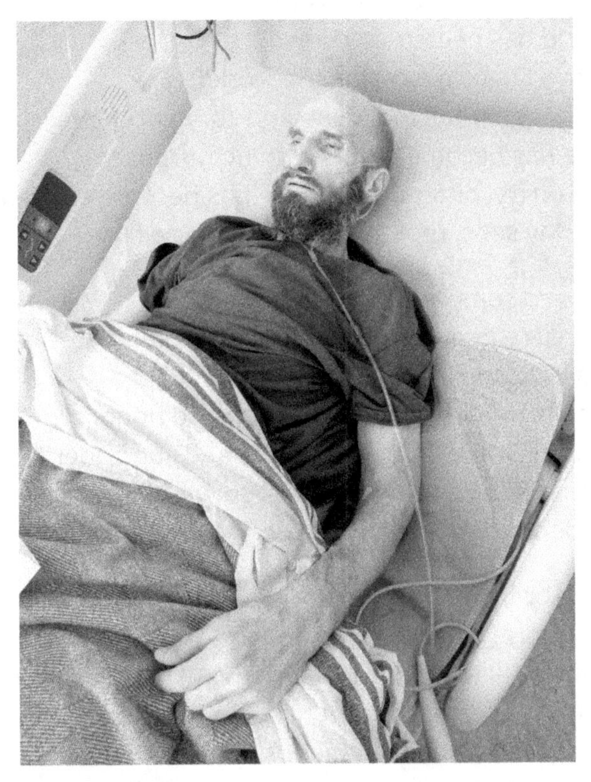

Sons of Adam

Awaken, sons of Adam, awaken
The world has beaten you down,
But know, I have overcome the world!
Arise, enough living in defeat, and complacency
Your life has become empty with no purpose
You are angry, bitter and offence has become epidemic
Repent, My sons, repent and deny yourself

My beloved sons, arise
You were created to lead, to have dominion of the earth
To be a beacon of love and grace to mankind
Rise up and lead My people in truth and honor
I Am calling you to bend your knee and surrender all
Your life is to be a living sacrifice, so walk in freedom
Stand, deny yourself and take up the Cross

Sons of Abraham, be in one accord
Fear My Holy Name, and rest in Me
Diligently seek to know My heart, the works of My hands
Walk in My power and authority
Be strengthened, be courageous, be bold
For I Am with you always, and will supply all your needs
Stand firm, deny yourself, pick up the Cross and follow ME

Beloved sons of the Lord Most High
The battle is raging, time to fight, be My warriors
I AM your rock, your fortress, your shield
Nothing can separate you from Me

You can do all things, and even greater works through Christ
Be My love and shepherd My people
Walk in victory for I AM the Alpha and Omega

***

We soon realized there was no time to try any therapy. The only thing that could save Ken was a miracle. Ken steadily got worse and ended up in palliative care at our local hospital. Ken had spent almost four months in a lot of pain and with little sleep, and he was so tired, that he told me he wanted to die. I told him to just hang on a few more days. We needed him and he had to fight because he couldn't let the enemy win. I didn't want to lose Ken. Sadness filled Ken's face. We were expecting pastoral friends in two days, and they were coming from a distance, to surround Ken in Father's love and prayer. They came and blessed us so much and in talking with our pastor I realized that I had been wrong. Whether Ken lived or died, the enemy couldn't win, for he can take the body but never the soul. So if Ken died, it would be a win – he would go to heaven to be with his Lord.

So I apologized to Ken, and told him that in dying he was victorious! The look of joy on his face melted my heart. I loved him so much and didn't want to lose him. I still, however, believed in a miracle healing.

The next day I asked our friends to bring juice and bread so we could partake in communion together. Ken was getting weaker and he'd lost so much weight. I continued to touch Ken, holding his hand, rubbing his feet, anything to help make him more comfortable. Even when I slept in the chair I tried to be close enough to be able to touch Ken throughout the night. We played worship music and if I awoke during the night, I prayed and sang over Ken. I believed Abba Father was going to heal Ken completely, but I had hoped it would be here on earth. And Abba Father did, just not on earth like I'd hoped. Early Friday morning, November 29, 2024 after I'd been praying and singing, Father took Ken to heaven where he was fully restored!

Ken was with Jesus!

The Lord is my shepherd;
I shall not want.
He makes me to lie down in green pastures;
He leads me beside the still waters.
He restores my soul;
He leads me in the paths of righteousness
For His name's sake.
Yea, though I walk through the valley of the shadow of death,
I will fear no evil;
For You are with me;
Your rod and Your staff, they comfort me.
You prepare a table before me in the presence of my enemies;
You anoint my head with oil;
My cup runs over.
Surely goodness and mercy shall follow me
All the days of my life;
And I will dwell in the house of the Lord
Forever.
Psalm 23:1-6

O How He Loves Us

My beloved sons and daughters
Your love has grown cold, your hearts hard
You are more concerned about yourselves and your wounds
I created you with purpose, to be the light of the world
But your light is barely a flicker
Awaken dear ones, awaken

My wayward children
Your offence and unforgiveness has become epidemic
Christ sacrificed all so you can live
Yet you reject Him over and over again in living
your life self-centered
You chose to live in misery, a prison of your own making
Repent sons, repent daughters and deny yourselves

A plan was weaved throughout My word,
for your redemption
From the beginning We had a way to make things right
For Christ to leave heaven and be born as a baby,
To grow to manhood and shed His blood to reconcile you
back into fellowship
To be the perfect sacrifice, and have victory over death!
O how We love you

Christ sacrificed everything to save you
He left power and glory to be born a helpless child
He was vulnerable and dependent totally on Me
He trusted Me to watch over Him
Christ obeyed Me unto death on the Cross
O how We love you

He suffered rejection throughout His life,
and yet Jesus loved them
Jesus was betrayed by His own people, and He loved them
Jesus was mocked and beaten, and He never
stopped loving them!
My Son was scourged beyond recognition, for you!
He chose to fulfill the Scriptures, because He loved them
and He loves you!
In your trials will you love them or grumble and curse them?

Jesus was crucified a criminals death, in love He forgave them
To redeem you, Jesus allowed them to mock,
beat and torture Him!
Through it all, He could have called 12 legions of angels
to save Himself
But He chose to walk in obedience
If Christ Jesus chose to love all, no matter
how they treated Him
How then can you reject Him who saved you,
to focus on yourselves?

My beloved, sons and daughters, life is a gift
Focusing on self is bondage, but looking to Christ is freedom!
I created you to live in victory, to be filled with peace and joy
To walk empowered, overflowing with My love
Surrender all, and let your light shine like the Son
Deny yourselves, take up the Cross and follow Me

In those months as Ken was fighting to live, Abba Father revealed His heart to us, especially to Ken. Through my love and the love of His people, Ken felt loved like he'd rarely felt before. It healed his broken heart and Ken died in freedom and in victory.

Another thing the Lord taught me was the importance of tears. They are like talents for the glory of God and not to be buried. I was trying so hard to be strong for Ken, not realizing that more tears would have promoted more healing. Not only for me but for us as a couple. Beloved, don't hold back your tears, they are a gift from God. It's how He moves us, revealing a contrite heart, a sign of great love, sincerity and a softened heart. If we hold back our tears our hearts can become hardened.

This next poem is about the vision from God given to our pastor while leading worship a couple weeks after Ken's death. Thank You Lord God for redeeming Ken's life even in death. Ken was crying out, super happy, joyful yet sobbing, and groaning from the depth of his being, a message for us all, "You need to tell them of the beauty of Jesus' scars!"

December 3rd, 2023. This was our last trip together to Vancouver Island. We have a lot of memories going to this beach. This is one of the last photos of us together.

The Beauty of Jesus' Scars

Beloved sons, beloved daughters hear My message!
Ken's voice is calling out **"O the beauty of His scars!"**
My Son willingly gave His life so you may live in freedom
Jesus shed his blood, He allowed man to torture Him
He was beaten, and scourged beyond recognition for you!
"O the beauty of Jesus' scars!"

My creation, I formed you, designed you with purpose
Hear Ken's voice cry out, like in the story of
the rich man in hell
But this warning comes from heaven to My bride
"You need to tell them about the beauty of His scars!"
**"How will they know the meaning of Jesus' wounds
without you telling them?"**
"O the beauty of the scars on Jesus' hands!"

Repent sons, repent daughters for time is fleeting
I AM calling you, you have forgotten you were
bought with a price
**"Don't waste your days away just surviving, there is
so much more!"**
"Don't miss out and wait until it's too late to tell them!"
You will stand before Me, what have you done
with what you knew?
"O the beauty of the scars on Jesus' feet!"

Awake O sleeper! O My bride, awaken!
Diligently pursue Me, strive to know My heart
Jesus loved you in your sin, and they are
washed away, forgotten

By looking upon the scars all guilt and shame fall away
Hunger to know the beauty of Jesus' scars and
let it transform you
Cry out beloved to see His scars!

My beloved, close your eyes, imagine Jesus before you
Touch His hands, his feet where the spikes tore through
Feel the rough and bumpy texture of His mutilated body
Every scar throughout Jesus's body was an act of love
Let My love embrace you, touch you to the very
depth of your soul
Beloved cry out, behold the beauty of Christ Jesus' scars!

✴✴✴

Into Your hand I commit my spirit;
You have redeemed me, O Lord God of truth.
Psalm 31:5

Greater love has no one than this, than to lay down one's life for
his friends.
John 15:13

"How then shall they call on Him in whom they have not believed?
And how shall they believe in Him of whom they have not heard?"
Romans 10:14

Losing Ken was very difficult. My heart was broken, but I know Abba Father IS Good and Faithful. His will is perfect. He knows what is best for us. Even though I miss Ken so much, I am so thankful that he is at perfect peace with Jesus. How could I take that away from him? I am so thankful for the time I had with Ken and I'm a better woman for having known him. We had our struggles, but it's in those times that we grow if we choose to. There were many blessings through this journey, especially that we ended well. It was like we fell in love with each other all over again, but much more deeply. I'm so thankful that we had those months together, no matter how hard they were. It was a time that brought healing into our lives, how God's people rallied around us with such love and support. Through that we got to know the Father's love more deeply. Neither Ken nor I had felt love like this in a long time, nor the peace and freedom. In spite of all our brokenness and everything that came against us, we stayed together over 34 years and loved each other more in the end.

One thing we learned is that we tend to be so hard on ourselves. We tend to focus too much on our failures, instead of our loving Father. Yes we make mistakes, but it doesn't mean our lives aren't touching people around us. There was a time when Ken questioned if he died would anyone even care? Father knows our hearts, our lives mean so much more than we realize! The Holy Spirit has been revealing to me how much Ken had impacted the people around him. Ken loved the Lord and longed to serve Him, but struggled with the lie that he was not good enough. Ken had such a way with people that Father's love even shone through in Ken's brokenness. Seeds were planted, and those that are dormant will take root, even after Ken's death, for the Lord is our Redeemer. Sometimes we walk this journey without seeing or recognizing the fruit we bear. Abba Father knew his heart. Even in his brokenness there was still a flicker of light.

Months later, I had the opportunity to go through deliverance to deal with the strongholds in my own life. This brought some things to light. The little girl in me had been trapped in darkness and hidden behind a veil, unseen. I was traumatized in my childhood and some memories had been blocked out. I hadn't realized how much fear I had been internalizing since my childhood. So many things now made sense. Through our church's leadership team, I was able to take that little girl who was trapped inside, wrap her in a robe, take her into my arms, and free her from her terror by bringing her out of darkness and into healing light. A few days later as I was meditating, Jesus gave me a gift. It was a picture of me, the little girl, curled up on Jesus' lap and He was stroking my hair. I looked up at Jesus with the biggest smile, then I sat up and threw my arms around Him, telling Jesus I loved Him. I slid off His lap and started to dance and skip, so carefree! Then I'm transformed from myself as a child to an adult and I'm joyfully walking beside Jesus.

Beloved, Abba Father wants each of you to be free, to live life to the fullest. Yes there have been, and will be, hardships but you are never alone. He will give you everything you need. Rest in Father's love and mercy and be filled with His peace and joy.

Beloved, choose *life*.

As I look back over the year since Ken passed. I am thankful that I got to spend over 34 years with Ken. One thing the Lord impressed upon me is to be thankful in all circumstances, not just in some but in all! I have a lot of wonderful memories from those years. It was not easy at times, sometimes very difficult, and at other times I wanted to throttle him! I'm sure he felt the same way about me at times! But as I think about all the years together, it was not about having our own needs met. We were not created to be served but rather to serve each other. It's about walking this journey, shoulder to shoulder, resting in Father to work all things out in us, for us and through us. For only the Father can truly meet our needs. Living loved is looking to the cross, denying ourselves and following Christ who has all things in His hands.

It was an honor to walk with Ken throughout those years. Ken loved the Lord and is now blessed to be in His presence. Ken is at peace, filled with joy, fully transformed by the Father's love. Thank You Lord, for loving us and loving Ken so much that he could finish the race. Our marriage and our covenant is completed; it is finished and we did well.

Farewell Ken, my handsome one, my love. I look forward to one day meeting again when I finish the race. To embrace, resting my head on your shoulder and walking side by side as you bring me to the Darling, the Wonder of heaven, to fully know, to understand the beauty of Jesus' scars.

My Bride

O My beloved bride, My children
I hear your cries, I have collected your tears
Turn away from the pain, the hurts of this world
THERE is NO shame, guilt or condemnation with ME
Your sins are washed away, forgotten!
Lay your burdens down, and rest in Me
My beloved sons, daughters, come to Me

My beloved creation, I Love you
You are chosen, created for such a time
I wove you in your mother's womb
Your life is written in My Book
I have a plan where you will prosper
My beloved believe, and I will provide all your needs
Children, My adopted heirs, awaken!

My cherished bride
Time is fleeting, the harvest is ready
Plow the ground, prepare for your future
Don't hold back, arise in divine courage
Let your actions display My love!
My beautiful bride, choose wisely
Deny yourself, take up the Cross and follow Me!

My precious children
You are in the palm of My hand, let My peace surround you
I see your heart and desire to serve
Walk in My boldness, My strength, My power and authority
Holy Spirit is My gift to you, surrender and He will guide you

Beloved, the time is now, come together
and walk in one accord.
My beautiful creation, be a blessing to all

My beautiful bride
Rise up, walk in freedom and be transformed
Just Loving me is not enough, you need to fear My Holy Name
Humble yourselves, bow before the throne, and repent
I created the heavens and the earth,
breathed life into existence
Fear Me, who can destroy both body and soul to hell
My children, holy reverence is the beginning of wisdom

Sons, daughters of the High King
You are redeemed, bought with the shedding of blood!
Run the race before you, and praise My Holy Name
Surrender, My children, yield to me and walk in obedience
Praise My Holy Name, fast and pray
Prepare, My blessed children, prepare for your future
Stand beloved and be My warriors

Rejoice, My children rejoice!
For you were lost and now are found
For nothing can separate Me from you
Walk empowered, with thanksgiving flowing from your lips
In knowing My word, you will know My heart
You are chosen, redeemed, My masterpiece
My beloved bride, take My hand and choose life

***

"Then the kingdom of heaven shall be likened to ten virgins who took their lamps and went out to meet the bridegroom. Now five of them were wise, and five were foolish. Those who were foolish took their lamps and took no oil with them, but the wise took oil in their vessels with their lamps. But while the bridegroom was delayed, they all slumbered and slept.

And at midnight a cry was heard: 'Behold, the bridegroom is coming; go out to meet him!' Then all those virgins arose and trimmed their lamps. And the foolish said to the wise, 'Give us some of your oil, for our lamps are going out.' But the wise answered, saying, 'No, lest there should not be enough for us and you; but go rather to those who sell, and buy for yourselves.'

And while they went to buy, the bridegroom came, and those who were ready went in with him to the wedding; and the door was shut.

Afterward the other virgins came also, saying, 'Lord, Lord, open to us!' But he answered and said, 'Assuredly, I say to you, I do not know you.'

Watch therefore, for you know neither the day nor the hour in which the Son of Man is coming."

Matthew 25:1-13

*Let us be glad and rejoice and give Him glory, for the marriage of
the Lamb has come, and His wife has made herself ready. "And
to her it was granted to be arrayed in fine linen, clean and bright,
for the fine linen is the righteous acts of the saints.*

*Then he said to me, "Write: 'Blessed are those who are called to
the marriage supper of the Lamb!' " And he said to me,
"These are the true sayings of God."*
Revelation 19:7-9

*"And behold, I am coming quickly, and My reward is with Me, to
give to every one according to his work. I am the Alpha and the
Omega, the Beginning and the End,
the First and the Last."*

*Blessed are those who do His commandments, that they may
have the right to the tree of life, and may enter through
the gates into the city.*

*"I, Jesus, have sent My angel to testify to you these things in the
churches. I am the Root and the Offspring of David,
the Bright and Morning Star."*

*And the Spirit and the bride say, "Come!" And let him who hears
say, "Come!" And let him who thirsts come. Whoever desires, let
him take the water of life freely.*
Revelation 22:12-14, 16-17

The Road Less Travelled

Enter by the narrow gate; for wide is the gate and broad is the way that leads to destruction, and there are many who go in by it. Because narrow is the gate and difficult is the way which leads to life, and there are few who find it."

Matthew 7:13-14

Beloved, Choose Life...

Holy, Holy, Holy
Is the Lord God Almighty
Praise Your Holy Name
May Your Kingdom come
Your Will be done
On Earth as it is in Heaven
Praise the Lord O My soul
For you are good and merciful
Your loving-kindness is better than life
The works of Your hands
Declare Your Holy Name
May every knee bow
And every tongue confess
Jesus Christ is Lord
May we all cry out together Abba Father!
Hallelujah, Hallelujah, Hallelujah
Amen, Amen, Amen

"That if you confess with your mouth the Lord Jesus and believe in your heart that God has raised Him from the dead, you will be saved."
Romans 10:9-10

"But God demonstrates His own love toward us, in that while we were still sinners, Christ died for us."
Romans 5:8

"For God so loved the world that He gave His only begotten Son, that whoever believes in Him should not perish but have everlasting life. For God did not send His Son into the world to condemn the world, but that the world through Him might be saved."
John 3:16-17

In Him you also trusted, after you heard the word of truth, the gospel of your salvation; in whom also, having believed, you were sealed with the Holy Spirit of promise, who is the guarantee of our inheritance until the redemption of the purchased possession, to the praise of His glory.
Ephesians 1:13-14

Therefore He says: "Awake, you who sleep, Arise from the dead, And Christ will give you light."
Ephesians 5:14

***

Lord Jesus, I have sinned. I believe You Lord Jesus are the Son of God. You died for my sins and God raised You from the dead. Forgive me Jesus for all of my sins. I invite you into my heart, my life, I surrender to You Lord Jesus. Thank You for dying on the cross for me, for saving me, for loving me. Thank you for the gift of the Holy Spirit to guide my way.

Welcome Beloved!

For you were lost but now are found!

Rejoice!

You are Home!

In Loving Memory

Ken enjoyed playing (and watching) many sports - from football to baseball and hockey - but hockey was his favorite and he played on and off throughout the years. He was an avid reader and loved music; he had built up quite a collection of various artists. Ken also loved people and made friends wherever he went. Ken took the time to visit at job sites, hardware stores, or

anywhere you bumped into him. Leona knew when Ken was late he was having a good visit somewhere.

In between his years of drywalling, Ken spent several years pastoring. This is when Ken's love for people shone through. Visiting and hospitality were a priority. As a child Ken remembered many Sundays when his mom had something in the oven ready so that missionaries, or other guests would be invited into their home where they enjoyed stories and lively conversations. This had a huge impact on his life.

Ken was also a gifted speaker and teacher. He enjoyed seeing the light of understanding God's truth come into someone's eyes. Even as time was running out and Ken was suffering, he still took the time to listen to people and encourage them by speaking blessing into their lives.

Ken Klassen died November 29, 2024 at 59 years old. Ken

loved the Lord. He was a family man who loved Leona and their four children. He was hardworking and dedicated to doing his job well. Ken is loved and so missed.

This was one of Ken's favourite passages:

I am the true vine, and My Father is the vinedresser. Every branch in Me that does not bear fruit He takes away; and every branch that bears fruit He prunes, that it may bear more fruit. You are already clean because of the word which I have spoken to you. Abide in Me, and I in you. As the branch cannot bear fruit itself, unless it abides in the vine, neither can you, unless you abide in Me.

I am the vine, you are the branches. He who abides in Me, and I in him, bears much fruit; for without Me you can do nothing. If anyone does not abide in Me, he is cast out as a branch and is withered; and they gather them and throw them into the fire, and they are burned. If you abide in Me, and My words abide in you, you will ask what your desire, and it shall be done for you. By this My Father is glorified, that you bear much fruit; so you will be My disciples.
John 15:1-8

You have turned for me my mourning into dancing;
You have put off my sackcloth and clothed me with gladness,
To that end that my glory may sing praise to You
and not be silent.
O Lord my God, I will give thanks to You forever.
Psalm 30:11-12

From The Author

Beloved sons, daughters of the Lord God Almighty.

Abba Father is calling us, the scattered stones, the remnant to know His heart; to awaken and rise up, and walk in one accord as His Church. We have lost our first love, allowed distractions, complacency and fear to creep into our lives and render us fruitless, dead. Our light has grown dim, barely a flicker in the darkness, but His light is still present.

Awaken, O sleepers, Awaken!
Be renewed, Be restored, Be redeemed!
Bring Heaven to earth, Be My light to the world!
My bride, it is time to prepare!
Be My Love!

Will you obey the call to seek and know Abba Father's heart, and to walk out your life surrendered to Him?

***

Then Jesus said to His disciples, "If anyone desires to come after Me, let him deny himself, and take up his cross , and Follow Me.
Matthew 16:24

Acknowledgements

Throughout this journey there have been many people who walked with Ken and I who brought such joy to our lives. There were many friends, neighbors and family who stood with us in those last months and with me after Ken passed, even from people we didn't know very well. Thank you! Words cannot express our gratitude for all of your love, support, prayers and kindness!

I want to thank several ladies who spent much time just being there, listening and helping me to have fun and laugh again. Your love and support will always be remembered and treasured! I want to thank those ladies who also helped and encouraged me with the beginnings of this book. It meant more than you know.

One of these ladies is my oldest friend who I've known since high school. I don't think I could fully describe her support during this time, because it touched me so deeply. Thank you for taking time to help me proofread and clarify my thoughts in completing this book. I am so blessed! Thank you!

I also want to thank my publishing and marketing consultant for her kindness, patience and expertise in working with me to get this book published. Thank you, I couldn't have done it without you!

May God bless you all for your kindness!

In You, O Lord, I put my trust;
Let me never be ashamed;
Deliver me in Your righteousness.
Bow down Your ear to me,
Deliver me speedily;
Be my rock of refuge,
A fortress of defence to save me.

For You are my rock and my fortress;
Therefore, for Your name sake,
Lead me and guide me.
Pull me out of the net which they have secretly laid for me,
For You are my strength.
Into Your hand I commit my spirit;
You have redeemed me,
O Lord God of truth.
Psalm 31:1-5

www.ingramcontent.com/pod-product-compliance
Lightning Source LLC
Chambersburg PA
CBHW071448030726

47593CB00003B/943